*Man's War
Against Nature*

Man's War Against Nature

RACHEL CARSON

PENGUIN BOOKS — GREEN IDEAS

PENGUIN BOOKS

UK | USA | Canada | Ireland | Australia
India | New Zealand | South Africa

Penguin Books is part of the Penguin Random House group of companies
whose addresses can be found at global.penguinrandomhouse.com.

Penguin
Random House
UK

First published in *Silent Spring* 1962
This extract published in Penguin Books 2021

001

Copyright © Rachel Carson, 1962

Set in 12.2/15pt Dante MT Std
Typeset by Jouve (UK), Milton Keynes
Printed and bound in Great Britain by Clays Ltd, Elcograf S.p.A.

The authorized representative in the EEA is Penguin Random House Ireland,
Morrison Chambers, 32 Nassau Street, Dublin D02 YH68

A CIP catalogue record for this book is available from the British Library

ISBN: 978–0–241–51445–0

www.greenpenguin.co.uk

There was once a town in the heart of America where all life seemed to be in harmony with its surroundings. The town lay in the midst of a checkerboard of prosperous farms, with fields of grain and hillsides of orchards, where white clouds of bloom drifted above the green land. In autumn, oak and maple and birch set up a blaze of color that flamed and flickered across a backdrop of pines. Then foxes barked in the hills and deer crossed the fields, half hidden in the mists of the mornings. Along the roads, laurel, viburnum, and alder, great ferns and wild flowers delighted the traveller's eye through much of the year. Even in winter, the roadsides were places of beauty, where countless birds came to feed on the berries and on the seed heads of the dried weeds rising above the snow. The countryside was, in fact, famous for the abundance and variety of its bird life, and when the flood of migrants was pouring through in spring and fall, people came from great distances to observe them. Other people came to fish streams, which flowed clear and cold out of the hills and contained shady pools where trout lay. So it had been from the days, many years ago, when the first settlers raised their houses, sank their wells, and built their barns.

Then, one spring, a strange blight crept over the area, and everything began to change. Some evil spell had settled on the community; mysterious maladies swept the flocks of chickens, and the cattle and sheep sickened and died. Everywhere was the shadow of death. The farmers told of much illness among their families. In the town, the doctors were becoming more and more puzzled by new kinds of sickness that had appeared among their patients. There had been several sudden and unexplained deaths, not only among the adults but also among the children, who would be stricken while they were at play, and would die within a few hours. And there was a strange stillness. The birds, for example – where had they gone? Many people, baffled and disturbed, spoke of them. The feeding stations in the back yards were deserted. The few birds to be seen anywhere were moribund; they trembled violently and could not fly. It was a spring without voices. In the mornings, which had once throbbed with the dawn chorus of robins, catbirds, doves, jays, and wrens, and scores of other bird voices, there was now no sound; only silence lay over the fields and woods and marshes. On the farms, the hens brooded but no chicks hatched. The farmers complained that they were unable to raise any pigs; the litters were small, and the young survived only a few days. The apple trees were coming into bloom, but no bees droned among the blossoms, so there was no pollination and there would be no fruit. The roadsides were lined with brown and withered vegetation, and were silent, too, deserted by all living things. Even the streams were lifeless. Anglers no longer visited them, for all the fish had died. In the gutters under the eaves, and between the shingles of the roofs, a few patches of white granular powder could be seen; some weeks earlier this powder had been dropped, like snow, upon the roofs and the lawns, the fields and the streams. No witchcraft, no enemy action had snuffed out life in this stricken world. The people had done it themselves.

This town does not actually exist; I know of no community that has experienced all the misfortunes I describe. Yet every one of them has actually happened somewhere in the world, and many communities have already suffered a substantial number of them. A grim spectre has crept upon us almost unnoticed, and soon my imaginary town may have thousands of real counterparts. What is silencing the voices of spring in countless towns in America? I shall make an attempt to explain.

The history of life on earth is a history of the interaction of living things and their surroundings. To an overwhelming extent, the physical form and the habits of the earth's vegetation and its animal life have been molded and directed by the environment. Over the whole span of earthly time, the opposite effect, in which life modifies its surroundings, has been relatively slight. It is only within the moment of time represented by the twentieth century that one species – man – has acquired significant power to alter the nature of his world, and it is only within the past twenty-five years that this power has achieved such magnitude that it endangers the whole earth and its life. The most alarming of all man's assaults upon the environment is the contamination of the air, earth, rivers, and seas with dangerous, and even lethal, materials. This pollution has rapidly become almost universal, and it is for the most part irrecoverable; the chain of evil it initiates, not only in the world that must support life but in living tissues, is for the most part irreversible. It is widely known that radiation has done much to change the very nature of the world, the very nature of its life; strontium 90, released into the air through nuclear explosions, comes to earth in rain or drifts down as fallout, lodges in soil, enters into the grass or corn or wheat grown there, and, in time, takes up its abode in the bones of a human being, there to remain until his death. It is less well known that many man-made chemicals act in much the same way as radiation; they lie long in the soil, and enter into living organisms, passing from one to another. Or they may travel mysteriously by underground streams, emerging to combine, through the alchemy of air and sunlight, into new forms, which kill vegetation, sicken cattle, and work unknown harm on those who drink from once pure wells. As Albert

Schweitzer has said, 'Man can hardly even recognize the devils of his own creation.' It took hundreds of millions of years to produce the life that now inhabits the earth – aeons of time, in which that developing and evolving and diversifying life reached a state of adjustment to its surroundings. To be sure, the environment, rigorously shaping and directing the life it supported, contained hostile elements. Certain rocks gave out dangerous radiation; even within the light of the sun, from which all life draws its energy, there were short-wave radiations with power to injure. But given time – time not in years but in millennia – life adjusted, and a balance was reached. Time was the essential ingredient. Now, in the modern world, there is no time. The speed with which new hazards are created reflects the impetuous and heedless pace of man, rather than the deliberate pace of nature. Radiation is no longer merely the background radiation of rocks, the bombardment of cosmic rays, the ultraviolet of the sun, which existed before there was any life on earth; radiation is now also the unnatural creation of man's tampering with the atom. The chemicals to which life is asked to make its adjustment are no longer merely the calcium and silica and copper and the rest of the minerals washed out of the rocks and carried in rivers to the sea; they are also the synthetic creations of man's inventive mind, brewed in his laboratories and having no counterparts in nature. To adjust to these chemicals would require time on the scale that is nature's; it would require not merely the years of a man's life but the life of generations. And even this would be futile, for the new chemicals come in an endless stream; almost five hundred annually find their way into actual use in the United States alone. The figure is staggering and its implications are not easily grasped: five hundred new chemicals to which the bodies of men and all other living things are required somehow to adapt each year – chemicals totally outside the limits of biological experience.

Among the new chemicals are many that are used in man's war against nature. In the past decade and a half, some six hundred basic chemicals have been created for the purpose of killing insects, weeds, rodents, and other organisms described in the modern vernacular as 'pests.' In the form of sprays, dusts, and aerosols, these basic chemicals are offered for sale under several thousand different brand names – a highly bewildering array of poisons, confusing even to the chemist, which have the power to kill every insect, the 'good' as well as the 'bad,' to still the song of birds and to stop the leaping of fish in the streams, to coat the leaves with poison and to linger on in soil. It may prove to be impossible to lay down such a barrage of dangerous poisons on the surface of the earth without making it unfit for all life. Indeed, the term 'biocide' would be more appropriate than 'insecticide' – all the more appropriate because the whole process of spraying poisons on the earth seems to have been caught up in an endless spiral. Since the late nineteen-forties, when DDT began to be used widely, a process of escalation has been going on in which ever more toxic chemicals must be found. This has happened because insects, in a triumphant vindication of Darwin's principle of the survival of the fittest, have consistently evolved super-races immune to the particular insecticide used, and hence a deadlier one has always had to be developed – and then a deadlier one than that. It has happened also that destructive insects often undergo a 'flareback,' or resurgence, after spraying, in numbers greater than before. The chemical war is never won, and all life is caught in its crossfire.

Along with the possibility of the extinction of mankind by nuclear war, a central problem of our age is the contamination of man's total environment with substances of incredible potential for harm – substances that accumulate in the tissues of plants and animals, and even penetrate the germ cells, to shatter or alter the very material of heredity, upon which the shape of the future depends. Some would-be architects of our future look toward a time when we will be able to alter the human germ plasm by design. But we may easily be altering it now by inadvertence, for many chemicals, like radiation, bring about gene mutations. It is ironic to think that man may determine his own future by something so seemingly trivial as the choice of his insect spray. The results, of course, will not be apparent for decades or centuries. All this has been risked – for what? Future historians may well be amazed by our distorted sense of proportion. How could intelligent beings seek to control a few unwanted species of weeds and insects by a method that brought the threat of disease and death even to their own kind?

The problem whose attempted solution has touched off such a train of disaster is an accompaniment of our modern way of life. Long before the age of man, insects inhabited the earth – a group of extraordinarily varied and adaptable beings. Since man's advent, a small percentage of the more than half a million species of insects have come into conflict with human welfare, principally in two ways – as competitors for the food supply and as carriers of human disease. Disease-carrying insects become important where human beings are crowded together, especially when sanitation is poor, as in times of natural disaster or war, or in situations of extreme poverty and deprivation. As for insects that compete with man for food, they become important with the intensification of agriculture – the devotion of immense acreages to the production of a single crop. Such a system sets the stage for explosive increases in specific insect populations. Single-crop farming does not take advantage of the principles by which nature works; it is agriculture as an engineer might conceive it to be. Nature has introduced great variety into the landscape, but man has displayed a passion for simplifying it. Thus he undoes the built-in checks and balances by which nature holds the various species within bounds. One important natural check is a limit on the amount of suitable habitat for each species. Obviously, an insect that lives on wheat can build up its population to much higher levels on a farm devoted solely to wheat than on a farm where wheat is intermingled with crops to which the insect is not adapted. In all such circumstances, insect control of some sort is necessary and proper. But in the case of both types of insect – the disease-carrying and the crop-consuming – it is a sobering fact that massive chemical control has had only limited success, and even threatens to worsen the very conditions it is intended to curb.

Another aspect of the insect problem is one that must be viewed against a background of geological and human history – the spreading of thousands of different kinds of organisms from their native homes into new territories. This worldwide migration has been studied and graphically described by the British ecologist

Charles Elton in his recent book 'The Ecology of Invasions by Animals and Plants.' During the Cretaceous period, some hundred million years ago, flooding seas created many islands within continents, and living things found themselves confined in what Elton calls 'colossal separate nature reserves.' There, isolated from others of their kind, they developed large numbers of new species. When some of the land masses were joined again, about fifteen million years ago, these species began to move out into new territories – a movement that not only is still in progress but is now receiving considerable assistance from man. The importation of plants is the primary agent in the modern spread of species, for animals have almost invariably gone along with the plants – quarantine being a comparatively recent and never completely effective innovation. The United States government itself has imported approximately two hundred thousand species or varieties of plants from all over the world. Nearly half of the hundred and eighty-odd major insect enemies of plants in the United States are accidental imports from abroad, and most of them have come as hitchhikers on plants.

In new territory, out of reach of the natural enemies that kept down its numbers in its native land,
an invading plant or animal is able to increase
its numbers enormously. Realistically speaking,
it would seem that insect invasions, both those
occurring naturally and those dependent on
human assistance, are likely to continue indefi-
nitely. We are faced, according to Dr. Elton, 'with
a life-and-death need not just to find new tech-
nological means of suppressing this plant or that
animal' but to acquire the basic knowledge of
animal populations and their relations to their
surroundings that will 'promote an even balance
and damp down the explosive power of out-
breaks and new invasions.' Much of the necessary
knowledge is now available, but we do not use
it. Have we fallen into a mesmerized state that
makes us accept as inevitable that which is infe-
rior or detrimental, as though we had lost the will
or the vision to demand that which is good? Such
thinking, in the words of the American ecologist
Paul Shepard, 'idealizes life with only its head out
of water, inches above the limits of toleration of
the corruption of its own environment,' and he
goes on to ask, 'Why should we tolerate a diet of

weak poisons, a home in insipid surroundings, a circle of acquaintances who are not quite our enemies, the noise of motors with just enough relief to prevent insanity? Who would want to live in a world which is just not quite fatal?'

Yet such a world is pressed upon us. For the first time in history, virtually every human being is subjected to contact with dangerous chemicals from birth to death. In the less than two decades of their use, DDT and other synthetic pesticides have been thoroughly distributed over all but a few corners of the world. They have been recovered from many of the major river systems, and even from the streams of ground water flowing unseen through the earth. They have been found in soil to which they were applied a dozen years before. They have lodged in the bodies of fish, birds, reptiles, and domestic and wild animals to the point where it is now almost impossible for scientists carrying on animal experiments to obtain subjects free from such contamination. They have been found in fish in remote mountain lakes, in earthworms burrowing in soil, in the eggs of birds, and in man himself. These chemicals are now stored in the bodies of the vast majority of human beings, regardless of their age. They occur in mother's milk, and probably in the tissues of the unborn child.

All this has come about because of the prodigious growth of an industry for the production of synthetic chemicals with insecticidal properties. This industry is a child of the Second World War. In the course of developing agents of chemical warfare, some of the chemicals created in the laboratory were found to be lethal to insects. The discovery did not come by chance; insects were widely used to test chemicals as agents of death for man. In being man-made – by the ingenious laboratory manipulation of molecules, involving the substitution of atoms or the alteration of their arrangement – the new insecticides differ sharply from the simpler ones of prewar days. These were derived from naturally occurring minerals and plant products: compounds of arsenic, copper, lead, manganese, zinc, and other minerals; pyrethrum, from the dried flowers of chrysanthemums; nicotine sulphate, from some of the relatives of tobacco; and rotenone, from leguminous plants of the East Indies. What sets the new synthetic insecticides apart is their enormous biological potency. They can enter into the most vital processes of the body and change them in sinister and often deadly ways. Yet new chemicals are added to the list each year, and new uses are devised for them. Production of synthetic pesticides in the United States soared from 124,259,000 pounds in 1947 to 637,666,000 pounds in 1960 – more than a fivefold increase. In 1960, the wholesale value of these products was well over a quarter of a billion dollars. But in the plans and hopes of the industry this enormous production is only a beginning. A *Who's Who* of pesticides, therefore, is of concern to us all. If we are going to live so intimately with these chemicals – eating and drinking them, taking them into the very marrow of our bones – we had better know something about their power.

The *Who's Who* would certainly include some of the pesticides that were used before the Second World War. Chief among these is arsenic, which is still the basic ingredient of a variety of weed and insect killers. Arsenic is a mineral occurring widely in association with the ores of various metals, and, in very small amounts, in volcanoes, in the sea, and in spring water. Its relations to

man are varied and historic. Since many of its
compounds are tasteless, it has been a favorite
agent of homicide from long before the time of the
Borgias. It was also the first recognized elemen-
tary carcinogen (or cancer-causing substance),
being identified in chimney soot and linked to
cancer nearly two centuries ago by an English
physician. Epidemics of chronic arsenical poisoning involving whole populations over long
periods are on record. Arsenic-contaminated
environments have also caused sickness and death
among horses, cows, goats, pigs, deer, fishes, and
bees, but arsenical sprays and dusts are still widely
applied. In the arsenic-sprayed cotton country
of the southern United States, beekeeping as an
industry has nearly died out. Farmers using arsenic dusts over long periods have been afflicted
with chronic poisoning; livestock have been
poisoned by crop sprays or weed killers containing arsenic. 'It is scarcely possible . . . to handle
arsenicals with more utter disregard of the general health than that which has been practiced in
our country in recent years,' Dr. W. C. Hueper,
of the National Cancer Institute, an authority on
environmental cancer, has said. 'Anyone who

has watched the dusters and sprayers of arsenical insecticides at work must have been impressed by the almost supreme carelessness with which these poisonous substances are dispensed.'

The vast majority of modern insecticides fall into one of two large groups of chemicals. One group, represented by DDT, consists of the chlorinated hydrocarbons. The other consists of the organic phosphates, and is represented by the reasonably familiar malathion and parathion. All have one thing in common: they are built on a basis of carbon atoms, which are also the indispensable building blocks of life, and thus both groups are classed as 'organic.' Carbon is an element whose atoms have an almost infinite capacity for uniting with each other in chains and rings and various other configurations, and for becoming linked with atoms of other substances. Indeed, the incredible diversity of living creatures, from bacteria to whales, is due in large measure to this capacity of carbon. The complex protein molecule has the carbon atom as its basis, as have molecules of fat, carbohydrates, enzymes, and vitamins. So, too, have enormous numbers of nonliving things, for carbon is not necessarily a symbol of life. Some organic compounds are combinations of carbon and hydrogen. The simplest of these is methane, or marsh gas, which is formed in nature by the bacterial decomposition of organic matter under water. Mixed with air in certain proportions, it becomes the dreaded firedamp of coal mines. The structure of methane is beautifully simple – one carbon atom to which four hydrogen atoms have become attached. Chemists have discovered that it is possible to detach one or all of the hydrogen atoms and substitute other elements. For example, take away three hydrogen atoms and substitute chlorine atoms, and we have the anesthetic chloroform. Substitute chlorine atoms for all of the hydrogen atoms, and the result is carbon tetrachloride, the familiar cleaning fluid. These changes wrung upon the basic molecule of methane illustrate in the simplest possible terms what a chlorinated hydrocarbon is. They give little hint of the complexity of the chemical world of the hydrocarbons, or of the manipulations by which the organic chemist creates his infinitely varied materials. For instead of the methane molecule, with its single carbon atom, he may work with hydrocarbon molecules consisting of many carbon atoms, arranged in rings or chains, and with side chains or branches, any of which may hold to themselves with chemical bonds not merely atoms of hydrogen or chlorine but also a wide variety of chemical groups. By seemingly slight changes, the whole character of the substance is transformed.

DDT (short for dichloro-diphenyl-trichloro-ethane) was first synthesized by a German chemist in 1874, but its properties as an insecticide were not discovered until 1939. Almost immediately thereafter, it was hailed as a means of stamping out insect-borne disease and winning the farmers' war against crop destroyers overnight, and, in due course, the chemist who had discovered its ability to kill insects, Paul Müller, of Switzerland, won the Nobel Prize. DDT is now so universally used that in most minds it has taken on the harmless aspect of the familiar. Perhaps the myth of the harmlessness of DDT rests on the fact that one of its first uses was the wartime dusting of many thousands of soldiers, refugees, and prisoners, to combat lice. It is widely believed that since so many people came into extremely intimate contact with DDT and suffered no immediate ill effects, the chemical must certainly be an innocent one. This understandable misconception arises from the fact that – unlike other chlorinated hydrocarbons – DDT in powder form is not readily absorbed through the skin. It does penetrate readily when it is dissolved in oil, as it usually is. If it is swallowed, it is absorbed slowly through the digestive tract; it may also be absorbed through the lungs. Once DDT, which, like all the chlorinated hydrocarbons, is soluble in fat, has entered the body, it is stored largely in organs rich in fatty substances, such as the adrenals, the testes, and the thyroid, and relatively large amounts are also deposited in the liver, the kidneys, and the fat of the large, protective mesentery, the tissue that enfolds the intestines and attaches them to the body wall. This storage of DDT begins with the smallest conceivable intake, and the fatty storage depots act as biological magnifiers, so that an intake of as little as one-tenth of one part per million in the diet results in the storage of from ten to fifteen parts per million – a hundredfold increase, or more. These terms of reference, so commonplace to the chemist or the pharmacologist, are unfamiliar to most of us. One part in a million sounds like a very small amount – and so it is. But some substances are so potent that a minute quantity can bring about vast changes in the body. For example, as little as three parts of DDT per million has been found to inhibit an oxidative enzyme in the heart muscle of experimental animals. In other experiments, only five parts of DDT per million brought about necrosis, or disintegration, of the cells of the liver; only 2.5 parts of the closely related insecticides dieldrin and chlordane have the same effect. This is really not surprising. In the normal chemistry of the human body, too, there is just such a disparity between cause and effect. For example, a quantity of iodine as small as two ten-thousandths of a gram can spell the difference between health and disease. Because these small amounts of pesticides are cumulatively stored and, in general, are built up at a rate higher than that at which they are excreted, the threat of chronic poisoning and of degenerative changes of the liver and other organs is a real one.

Scientists are not sure how much DDT can be stored in the human body. Some believe that there is a ceiling beyond which absorption and storage cease. Others do not. For practical purposes, it is not particularly important which view is right. Storage in human beings has been well investigated, and we know roughly how much the average person is storing. According to various studies, individuals with no known exposure except the inevitable dietary one store from 5.3 parts per million to 7.4 parts per million; agricultural workers about 17.1 parts per million; and workers in insecticide plants as high as 648 parts per million. Potentially harmful amounts undoubtedly vary from individual to individual, and, in any case, harmful results may not occur for years. The chemists' ingenuity in devising insecticides long ago outstripped the biologists' knowledge of the way these poisons affect the living organism.

One of the most significant features of DDT and related chemicals is the way they are passed on from one organism to another through all the links of the food chains. Fields of alfalfa, say, are dusted with DDT; meal is later prepared from the alfalfa and fed to hens; the hens lay eggs that contain DDT. Or the hay, containing residues of from seven to eight parts per million, may be fed to cows. The DDT will turn up in the milk in the amount of about three parts per million, but in butter made from this milk the concentration may run to sixty-five parts per million. During the process of transfer, what started out as a very small amount of DDT may end as a heavy concentration. The poison may be passed on from mother to offspring. The presence of insecticide residues in human milk has been established by Food and Drug Administration scientists. This is probably not the breast-fed infant's first exposure, however; there is good reason to believe that he starts receiving toxic chemicals while he is still in the womb. In experimental animals, the chlorinated-hydrocarbon insecticides freely cross the barrier of the placenta, the traditional protective shield between the embryo and harmful substances in the mother's body. While the quantities so received by human infants would normally be small, they would not be unimportant, because children are more susceptible to poisoning than adults.

Chlordane, another chlorinated hydrocarbon, has all the unpleasant attributes of DDT, plus a few that are peculiarly its own. Its residues are long persistent in soil, on foodstuffs, and on surfaces to which it may be applied, yet it is also quite volatile, and poisoning by inhalation is a definite risk to anyone handling it or exposed to it. Chlordane takes advantage of all available portals in entering the body. A diet containing such a small amount of chlordane as 2.5 parts per million may eventually lead to storage of seventy-five parts per million in the fat. In 1950, Dr. Arnold J. Lehman, who is the chief pharmacologist of the Food and Drug Administration, described chlordane as 'one of the most toxic of insecticides,' adding, 'Anyone handling it could be poisoned.' To judge by the carefree liberality with which dusts for treating suburban lawns are laced with chlordane, this warning has not been taken to heart. If a suburbanite handling one of them is not instantly stricken, this does not mean he has escaped harm; the toxins may sleep long in his body, to become manifest months or years later in an obscure disorder that is almost impossible to trace to its origins. However, death may sometimes strike quickly. One man who accidentally spilled a twenty-five-per-cent solution of chlordane on his skin developed symptoms of poisoning within forty minutes and died before medical help could be obtained.

Heptachlor, one of the constituents of chlordane, is marketed as a separate formulation. It has a particularly high capacity for storage in fat. If the diet contains as little as a tenth of one part per million, there will be measurable amounts of heptachlor in the body. It also has the curious ability to undergo change into a chemically distinct substance known as heptachlor epoxide. It does this in soil and in the tissues of both plants and animals. Laboratory tests on quail show that the epoxide is from two to four times as toxic as the original chemical.

As long ago as the mid-nineteen-thirties, a special group of hydrocarbons, the chlorinated naphthalenes, had been found to cause hepatitis and a rare and almost invariably fatal disease known as yellow atrophy of the liver in persons subjected to occupational exposure. These chemicals have led to illness and death of workers in electrical industries (where they are used in insulation), and more recently, in agriculture, they have been considered a cause of a mysterious and usually fatal disease of cattle. It is not surprising that three of the insecticides that belong to this group are among the most violently poisonous of all the hydrocarbons. These are dieldrin, aldrin, and endrin.

Dieldrin, named for a German chemist, Otto Diels, is about five times as toxic as DDT when it enters the body through the mouth and forty times as toxic when it is absorbed through the skin in solution. It is notorious for striking quickly at the nervous system, sending the victim into convulsions. Because the insecticidal action of dieldrin is particularly potent, and because its residues persist for a long period, it is one of the most widely used insecticides today. There are vast gaps in our knowledge of how dieldrin is stored and distributed in the body, and of the extent to which it is excreted, but there are indications of long storage in the human body, where deposits may lie dormant like a slumbering volcano, only to flare up in periods of physiological stress, when the body draws upon its fat reserves. Much of what we do know has been learned through hard experience in the anti-malarial campaigns carried out by the World Health Organization.

As the malaria mosquitoes have become resistant to DDT, dieldrin has been substituted in malaria-control work, and, as this has happened, cases of poisoning have appeared among the spraymen. A study published in 1959 reported that the seizures were severe; from half to all of the men affected – the proportion varied in different programs – went into convulsions, and several died. Some were still subject to convulsions as long as four months after the last exposure.

Aldrin is a still more mysterious substance, for although it exists as a separate entity, it bears the relation of alter ego to dieldrin. When carrots are taken from a bed treated with aldrin, they are found to contain residues of dieldrin – a change that occurs both in the living tissues and in the soil. If a chemist, knowing that aldrin has been applied, tests for it, he will be deceived into thinking all residues have been dissipated. The residues are there, but they are dieldrin, and this requires a different test. In any event, aldrin is slightly more toxic than dieldrin. It has produced degenerative changes in the liver and kidneys of experimental animals. A quantity the size of an aspirin tablet is enough to kill more than four hundred quail.

Many cases of human poisoning are on record, most of them in connection with industrial handling. Beyond that, aldrin, like most of this group of insecticides, projects a menacing shadow into the future – the shadow of sterility. Birds that consume it in quantities too small to kill them lay few eggs, and the chicks that hatch soon die. Rats who have been exposed to aldrin have fewer pregnancies, and their young are sickly and short-lived, and puppies whose mothers have been exposed to the poison have been known to die within three days. By one means or another, the new generations suffer as a result of poisoning of their parents. No one knows whether the same effect will be seen in human beings.

The third of the naphthalenes, endrin, is perhaps the most toxic of all the chlorinated hydrocarbons now in use. Although it is chemically rather closely related to dieldrin, a little twist in its molecular structure makes it up to twelve times as poisonous to rats; by comparison, DDT seems almost harmless. In the decade of its use, endrin has killed enormous numbers of fish, has fatally poisoned cattle that have wandered into sprayed orchards, and has poisoned wells. At least one state health department has warned that careless use of endrin is endangering human lives. But even apparently careful use can be dangerous. In 1958, an American couple with a year-old boy had gone to live in Venezuela.. There were cockroaches in the house they moved into, and after a few days they used a spray containing endrin. The baby and the small family dog were taken out of the house before the spraying was done, about nine o' clock one morning. After the spraying, the floors were washed. The baby and dog were returned to the house in midafternoon. An hour or so later, the dog vomited, went into convulsions, and died. At ten in the evening, the baby also vomited and went into convulsions, and then lost consciousness. At once, this normal, healthy child became little more than a vegetable – unable to see or hear, subject to frequent muscular spasms, and, it would seem, completely cut off from his surroundings. Several months of treatment in a New York hospital failed to change his condition or bring hope of change. 'It is extremely doubtful,' reported the attending physicians, 'that any useful degree of recovery will occur.'

The second major group of insecticides, the organic phosphates – esters of phosphoric acid – are among the most poisonous chemicals in the world. The origin of these chemicals has a certain ironic significance. Some of them had been known for many years, but their insecticidal properties were first discovered by a German chemist, Gerhard Schrader, in the late nineteen-thirties. Almost at once, the German government recognized the value of these chemicals as new and devastating weapons in man's war against his own kind, and work on them was declared secret. Some became nerve gases. Others became insecticides. The chief and most obvious hazard attending their use is that of acute poisoning of people applying the sprays or accidentally coming in contact with drifting spray, or vegetation coated with it, or a discarded container. In Florida, in 1960, two children used a discarded bag to repair a swing. Shortly thereafter, both of them died, and three of their playmates became ill. The bag had once contained the insecticide parathion, and tests established death by parathion poisoning.

The organic-phosphate insecticides act on the living organism in a peculiar way. They have the ability to destroy enzymes – enzymes that perform necessary functions in the body. Their target, whether the victim is an insect or a warm-blooded animal, is the nervous system. Under normal conditions, an impulse passes from nerve to nerve with the aid of a 'chemical transmitter' called acetylcholine, a substance that performs an essential function and then disappears. Indeed, its existence is so ephemeral that without special procedures medical researchers are unable to sample it before the body has destroyed it. The transient nature of the chemical transmitter is necessary to the normal functioning of the body. If the acetylcholine is not inactivated as soon as a nerve impulse has passed, impulses continue to flash across the bridge from nerve to nerve; the chemical not only goes on exerting its effect but exerts it in an ever more intensified manner. The movements of the whole body become uncoordinated; tremors, muscular spasms, convulsions, and death quickly result. Fortunately, the body has its own protective device against this peril – an enzyme called cholinesterase, which breaks down the transmitting chemical once it is no longer needed. By this means, a precise balance is struck, and the body never builds up a dangerous amount of acetylcholine. But on contact with the organic-phosphate insecticides the activity of the protective enzyme is inhibited, and as the effective quantity of the enzyme is reduced, that of the chemical transmitter builds up. In having this effect, the organic-phosphate compounds resemble the alkaloid poison muscarine, found in a poisonous mushroom, the fly amanita. Repeated exposure may lower the cholinesterase level until an individual reaches the brink of acute poisoning – a brink over which he may be pushed by a very small additional exposure. For this reason, it is considered important to make periodic examinations of the blood of spray operators and others regularly exposed.

Parathion is one of the most widely used of the organic phosphates. It is also one of the most powerful. Honeybees become agitated and bellicose on contact with it, engage in frantic cleaning movements, and are near death within half an hour. A chemist, hoping to learn by the most direct means the dose acutely toxic to human beings, swallowed a minute amount, about .00424 of an ounce. Paralysis followed so swiftly that he could not reach the antidotes he had at hand, and so he died. One of the circumstances that save us from extinction by parathion and the other chemicals of the organic-phosphate group is that they are decomposed rather rapidly. However, they last long enough to create hazards and produce consequences that range from the merely serious to the fatal. In Riverside, California, eleven out of thirty men picking oranges became violently ill, and all but one of the eleven had to be hospitalized. The grove had been sprayed with parathion some two and a half weeks earlier; the residues that reduced them to retching, half-blind, semiconscious misery were from sixteen to nineteen days old. And this is not by any means a record for persistence. On citrus fruit, parathion has been found to have a 'half life' of from sixty to eighty days; in that amount of time, half the chemical disintegrates. The danger to all workers applying the organic-phosphate insecticides is so extreme that some states using these chemicals have established laboratories where physicians may obtain aid in diagnosis and treatment. The physicians themselves may be in some danger, unless they wear rubber gloves while they are handling the

victims of poisoning. So may a laundress wash-
ing a victim's clothing. Parathion is now said to
be a favorite instrument of suicide in Finland. In
recent years, the state of California has reported
an average of two hundred cases of accidental
parathion poisoning annually. In many parts
of the world, the fatality rate from parathion is
startling: a hundred fatal cases in India and sixty-
seven in Syria in 1958, and an average of three
hundred and thirty-six a year in Japan. Yet some
six million pounds of parathion are now applied
annually to fields, orchards, and vineyards of the
United States – by hand sprayers, by motorized
blowers and dusters, and by airplane. The amount
used on California farms alone could, according
to Dr. Irma West, of the California State Department of Public Health, 'provide a lethal dose for
five to ten times the whole world's population.'

Malathion is almost as familiar to the public as
DDT, being widely used in gardening, in house-
hold insecticides, in mosquito spraying, and in
such blanket attacks on insects as the spraying of
nearly a million acres in Florida for the Mediterranean fruit fly. It is considered the least toxic of
the organic phosphates, and many people assume

that they may use it freely. Actually, the alleged safety of malathion rests on rather precarious ground, although – as often happens – this was not discovered until the chemical had been in use for several years. Malathion is 'safe' only because the mammalian liver, an organ with extraordinary protective powers, renders it relatively harmless. The detoxication is accomplished by one of the enzymes of the liver. If, however, something destroys this enzyme or interferes with its action, the person exposed to malathion receives the full force of its toxic action, which resembles that of the other organic phosphates. Unfortunately for all of us, opportunities for this sort of thing to happen are legion. A few years ago, a team of Food and Drug Administration scientists discovered that when malathion and one of the other organic phosphates are administered simultaneously, a severe poisoning results – up to fifty times as severe as one would predict on the basis of adding together the toxicities of the two. In other words, one one-hundredth of the lethal dose of each compound can be fatal when the two are combined. This discovery led to the testing of other combinations, and, although the full scope of the interaction of chemicals has not yet been determined, it is now known that many pairs of organic-phosphate insecticides are similarly dangerous, the toxicity being 'potentiated,' or stepped up, through the combined action. Potentiation seems to take place when one compound destroys the liver enzyme responsible for detoxicating the other. The two need not be given simultaneously. And the hazard exists not only for the man who may spray this week with one insecticide and next week with another; it exists also for the consumer of sprayed products. The common salad bowl may easily present a combination of organic-phosphate insecticides in quantities large enough to interact.

In Greek mythology, the sorceress Medea, enraged at being supplanted by a rival in the affections of her husband, Jason, presented the new bride with a robe possessing magical properties. The wearer of the robe immediately suffered a violent death. This death-by-indirection now has its counterpart in what are known as 'systemic insecticides.' These are chemicals that are used to convert plants or animals into a sort of Medea's robe. The purpose is to kill insects that may come in contact with these poisonous beings, especially by sucking their juices or their blood. The world of systemic insecticides is a weird world, surpassing the imaginings of the brothers Grimm. It is a world where the enchanted forest of the fairy tales has become a poisonous forest. It is a world where a flea bites a dog and dies, where an insect may die as a result of chewing a leaf or inhaling vapors emanating from a plant it has never touched, where a bee may carry poisonous nectar back to its hive and presently produce poisonous honey.

The entomologists' dream of the built-in insecticide was born when workers in the field of applied entomology realized they could take a hint from nature: they found that wheat growing in soil that contains sodium selenate was poisonous to aphids. Selenium, a naturally occurring element found sparingly in rocks and soils of many parts of the world, thus became the first systemic insecticide. What makes an insecticide a systemic is its ability to permeate all the tissues of a plant or animal and make them toxic. This quality is possessed by some chemicals of the chlorinated-hydrocarbon group and by others of the organic-phosphate group, all synthetically produced. In practice, most systemics are drawn from the organic-phosphate group, because with these the problem of residues is somewhat less acute.

Systemics can act in devious ways. Applied to seeds, either by soaking or by means of a coating in which the systemic is combined with carbon, they extend their effects into the following plant generation and produce seedlings poisonous to aphids and other sucking insects. Such vegetables as peas, beans, and sugar beets are sometimes thus protected. Cotton seeds coated with a systemic called phorate have been in use for some time in California, and in 1959 twenty-five farm laborers in the San Joaquin Valley, who had handled bags of treated seeds, were seized with sudden illness. In England, someone wondered what happened when bees made use of nectar from plants that had been treated with systemics. This was investigated in areas treated with a chemical called schradan. Although the plants had been sprayed before the flowers were formed, the nectar they produced contained the poison. The result, as might have been predicted, was that the honey made by the bees was also contaminated with schradan.

Animal systemics have been used chiefly to control the cattle grub, a damaging parasite of livestock. Extreme care must be taken in order to create an insecticidal effect in the blood and tissues of the host without setting up a fatal poisoning. The balance is very delicate indeed, and government veterinarians have found that repeated small doses can gradually deplete an animal's supply of cholinesterase, so that without warning a minute additional dose will cause poisoning. As yet, no one seems to have proposed a human systemic that would make us lethal to a mosquito. Perhaps this is the next step.

When we turn our attention to herbicides, or weed killers, we quickly come across the legend that they are toxic only to plants. Unfortunately, this is only a legend. The plant killers include a large variety of chemicals that act on animal tissue as well as on vegetation. No general statement can describe the action of all of them. Some are general poisons; some are powerful stimulants of metabolism, causing a fatal rise in body temperature; some can induce malignant tumors, either alone or in partnership with other chemicals; some can cause gene mutations.

Arsenic compounds are still liberally used, both as insecticides and as weed killers, where they usually take the chemical form of sodium arsenite. The history of their use is not reassuring. As roadside sprays, they have cost many a farmer his cow and killed uncounted numbers of wild creatures. As aquatic weed killers, they have made public waters unsuitable for drinking, or even for swimming. As a spray applied to potato fields to destroy the vines, they have taken a toll of human and non-human life. In England, this last practice developed in about 1951, as a result of a shortage of sulphuric acid, which had formerly been used to burn off the potato vines. The Ministry of Agriculture considered it necessary to issue a warning of the hazard of going into arsenic-sprayed fields, but the warning was not understood by the cattle (or by the wild animals and birds), and reports of poisoned cattle were received with monotonous regularity. In 1959, after death came to a farmer's wife through arsenic-contaminated water, one of the major English chemical companies stopped production of arsenical sprays and called in supplies already in the hands of dealers, and shortly thereafter the Ministry of Agriculture announced that restrictions on the use of arsenites would be imposed. In 1961, the Australian government announced a similar ban. No such restrictions impede the use of these poisons in the United States.

The most widely used herbicides are 2,4-D, 2,4,5-T, and related members of what is known as the phenol group. Many experts deny that these are toxic. However, people spraying their lawns with 2,4-D and becoming wet with spray have occasionally developed severe neuritis and even paralysis. Although such incidents are apparently uncommon, medical authorities advise caution in the use of these compounds. Other hazards, more obscure, may also attend the use of 2,4-D. Experiments have shown its ability to disturb the basic physiological process of respiration in the cell, and, like X-rays, to damage the chromosomes. Some very recent work indicates that sub-lethal doses of these herbicides may affect reproduction in birds. The rest of the phenols may be equally dangerous. Dinitrophenol, for example, steps up the metabolism. For this reason, it was at one time used in the United States as a reducing drug, but the margin between the slimming dose and the dose required to poison or kill was slight – so slight that at least nine patients died and many suffered permanent injury before use of the drug was finally halted. It interferes with the body's source of energy in such a way that the affected organism almost literally burns itself up. A related chemical, pentachlorophenol, sometimes known as 'penta,' is used both as a weed killer and as an insecticide, often being sprayed along railroad tracks and in waste areas. The fearful power of penta, which acts in much the same way as dinitrophenol, is illustrated in a fatal accident recently reported by the California State Department of Public Health. A man was preparing a cotton defoliant by mixing diesel oil with penta. As he was drawing the concentrated chemical out of a drum, the spigot accidentally toppled back. He reached in with his bare hand to regain the spigot. Although he washed immediately, he became acutely ill, and died the next day.

Curious indirect results follow the use of certain herbicides. It has been found that animals – both wild herbivores and livestock – are sometimes strangely attracted to a plant that has been sprayed, even though it is not one of their natural foods. Apparently, the wilting that follows spraying (or cutting) makes the plant attractive. If a highly poisonous herbicide, such as arsenic, has been used, this intense desire to reach the wilting vegetation inevitably has disastrous consequences. Such consequences may also stem from the use of less toxic herbicides in cases where the plant itself happens to be poisonous or, perhaps, to possess thorns or burs. Poisonous range weeds, for example, have suddenly become attractive to livestock after spraying, and the animals have died from indulging this unnatural appetite. The literature of veterinary medicine abounds in similar examples: swine eating sprayed cockleburs with consequent severe illness, lambs eating sprayed thistles, bees poisoned by pasturing on mustard that had been sprayed after it came into bloom. Wild cherry, the leaves of which are highly poisonous, has had a fatal attraction for cattle once its foliage has been sprayed with 2,4-D. The explanation of this peculiar behavior sometimes appears to lie in the changes that the chemical brings about in the metabolism of the plant. There is a temporary but marked increase in sugar content, and many animals seek the plant out for its sweetness.

Another curious effect of 2,4-D has important consequences for livestock and wildlife, and apparently for men as well. Experiments carried out about a decade ago showed that after treatment with this chemical there is a sharp increase in the nitrate content of corn and of sugar beets, and that this might also be true of sorghum, sunflower, spiderwort, lamb's-quarters, pigweed, and smartweed. Some of these are normally ignored by cattle but are eaten with relish after treatment with 2,4-D. According to some agricultural specialists, a number of deaths among cattle have been traced to such sprayed weeds. All ruminants – not only cattle but wild ruminants, such as deer, antelope, sheep, and goats – have a digestive system of extraordinary complexity, including a stomach divided into several chambers. The digestion of cellulose is accomplished in one of the chambers, through the action of microorganisms known as rumen bacteria. When the animal feeds on vegetation containing nitrates, the rumen bacteria change them into nitrites, and if the level of nitrates is abnormally high, a fatal series of events ensues. When the nitrites are present in large quantities, they act on the blood pigment to form a chocolate-brown substance in which oxygen is so firmly held that it cannot be transferred from the lungs to the tissues. And death occurs within a few hours from anoxia, or lack of oxygen. Now it appears that the custom of spraying corn with 2,4-D may be a factor in the current increase in the number of 'silo deaths' – deaths of men who have entered silos where corn, oats, or sorghum containing large amounts of nitrates have released poisonous nitrogen oxide gases. So serious is the problem that the New York State Co-operative Extension Service recently issued a poster warning, 'Silo gases can kill you and your herd!' Although various factors, including exceptionally dry weather, can cause an increase in nitrate content, the effect of 2,4-D cannot be ignored. The situation was considered important enough by the University of Wisconsin Agricultural Experiment Station to justify a warning in 1957 that 'plants killed by 2,4-D may contain large amounts of nitrate.' Only a few breaths of one of the gases released by nitrates can cause a diffuse chemical pneumonia. In a series of cases studied by the University of Minnesota Medical School, all but one terminated fatally.

The pollution of our environment has many sources – radioactive wastes, fallout from nuclear explosions, domestic wastes from cities and towns, and chemical wastes from factories as well as the new fallout from chemical sprays – and it affects every one of man's natural resources. Of these, water has become the most precious. By far the greater part of the earth's surface is covered by its seas, yet in the midst of this plenty we are in want. Most of the earth's abundant water is not usable for agriculture, industry, or human consumption, because of its heavy load of salts, and so most of the world's population either is experiencing critical shortages of water or is threatened with them. And the water that is usable has become – in an age when man has forgotten his origins and is blind to the very conditions that are most essential to his survival – the victim of man's indifference.

Ever since chemists began to manufacture substances that nature never invented, the problems of water purification have grown more complex and the danger to users of water has increased. In rivers, a really incredible variety of pollutants is present, producing combined deposits that the sanitary engineers can only refer to despairingly as 'gunk.' Professor Rolf Eliassen of the Massachusetts Institute of Technology testified before a congressional committee to the impossibility of identifying the organic matter resulting from the mixture. 'We don't know what that is,' said Professor Eliassen. 'What is the effect on people? We don't know.' We do know one thing, and that is that to an ever-increasing degree pesticides contribute to these organic pollutants. Because they become inextricably mixed with domestic and other wastes, they sometimes defy detection by the standard methods used in purification plants. Often they cannot be identified, and even if they are, most of them are so stable that they cannot be broken down by ordinary processes. Some are deliberately applied to bodies of water to destroy plants, insect larvae, or undesired fish. Some come from forest spraying, in the course of which two or three million acres of one of our states may be blanketed with spray directed against a single insect pest – spray that falls directly into streams or else drips down through the leafy canopy to the forest floor, there to become part of the slow movement of seeping moisture beginning its long journey to the sea. Probably the bulk of such contaminants, however, consists of water-borne residues of the millions of pounds of agricultural chemicals that have been leached out of the ground by rains to become part of the same seaward movement.

Here and there we have dramatic evidence of the presence of these chemicals in our streams, and even in public water supplies. A sample of drinking water from an orchard area in Pennsylvania was tested on fish in a laboratory; it contained enough insecticide to kill all the fish within four hours, The runoff from fields treated with a chlorinated hydrocarbon called toxaphene killed all the fish in fifteen streams tributary to the Tennessee River, in Alabama, two of which were sources of municipal water supplies; the water remained poisonous for a week after the application of the insecticide – a fact that was determined by the daily deaths of goldfish suspended in cages downstream. For the most part, such pollution is invisible; it may make its presence known when hundreds or thousands of fish die, but more often it is never detected at all.

Anyone who doubts that our waters have become almost universally contaminated with insecticides might well study a brief report issued by the United States Fish and Wildlife Service in 1960. The Service had carried out studies to discover whether fish, like warm-blooded animals, store insecticides in their tissues. The first samples were taken from a creek in a forest area in the West where there had been mass spraying of DDT for the control of the spruce budworm. As might have been expected, all these fish contained DDT. The really significant findings were made when the investigators turned for comparison to a remote creek thirty miles from the nearest area sprayed for budworm control. This creek was upstream from the first, and separated from it by a high waterfall. No local spraying was known to have occurred. Yet the fish in that creek, too, contained DDT. Had the chemical been airborne, drifting down as fallout on the surface of the creek? Or had it reached the creek by hidden underground streams?

Probably no aspect of the entire water-pollution problem is more disturbing than the threat of widespread contamination of ground water. Seldom if ever does nature operate in separate compartments, and she has not done so in distributing the earth's water supply. As rain falls on the land, it seeps down through pores and cracks in soil and rock, penetrating deeper and deeper, until eventually it reaches a zone where all the pores of the bedrock are filled with water – a dark, subsurface sea, rising under hills, sinking beneath valleys. This ground water is always on the move, sometimes as slowly as fifty feet a year, sometimes as rapidly as nearly a tenth of a mile in a day. It travels unseen until, here and there, it comes to the surface as a spring, or perhaps is tapped to feed a well. But mostly it contributes invisibly to streams, and so to rivers. Except for the water that enters streams directly as rain or surface runoff, all the running water on the earth's surface was at one time ground water. And so pollution of the ground water is pollution of water everywhere.

It must have been by such a dark underground sea that poisonous chemicals travelled from a manufacturing plant in Colorado to a farming district several miles away. What happened, in brief, is this. In 1943 the Rocky Mountain Arsenal of the Army Chemical Corps, situated near Denver, began to manufacture war materials. Eight years later, the facilities of the arsenal were leased to a private oil company for the production of insecticides. Even before the changeover, however, mysterious reports had begun to come in. Farmers several miles from the plant reported unexplained sickness among livestock, and they complained of extensive crop damage; foliage turned yellow, plants failed to mature, and many crops were killed outright. And there were reports of human illness. The waters used for the irrigation of these farms were derived from shallow wells. In 1959, a study was undertaken, in which several state and federal agencies participated, and when the well waters were examined they were found to contain an assortment of chemicals. Such wastes as chlorides, chlorates, salts of phosphonic acid, fluorides, and arsenic had been discharged from the Rocky Mountain Arsenal during the years of its operation by the Army Chemical Corps. It was concluded that some of these wastes had found their way into the ground water at the arsenal and that it had taken from seven to eight years for them to travel underground a distance of about three miles from two of the arsenal's original holding ponds – mere depressions in the earth, into which wastes were discharged – to the nearest farm. The investigators knew of no way to contain the contamination – to halt its advance. All this was bad enough, but the most mysterious and probably, in the long run, the most significant feature of the whole episode was the discovery of 2,4-D in the holding ponds of the arsenal, even though no 2,4-D had been manufactured there during any stage of operations. After long and careful study, the chemists at the plant concluded that the 2,4-D had been formed spontaneously in the holding ponds, from other substances discharged from the arsenal; in the presence of catalyzing air and sunlight, and quite without the intervention of human chemists, the ponds had become laboratories for the production of a new chemical.

Indeed, one of the most alarming aspects of the chemical pollution of water is the fact that in river or lake or reservoir – or, for that matter, in the glass of water served at your dinner table – are mingled chemicals that no responsible chemist would think of combining in his laboratory. The possible interactions between these chemicals, often comparatively harmless in themselves, are deeply disturbing to officials of the United States Public Health Service. The reactions may take place between two or more chemicals, or between various chemicals and radioactive wastes. Under the impact of ionizing radiation, rearrangements of atoms could easily occur, changing the nature of the chemical in a wholly unpredictable way, and one that would be wholly beyond control.

A striking example of the contamination of surface waters seems to be building up in the National Wildlife Refuges at Tule Lake and Lower Klamath Lake, both in California. These refuges are part of a group, which also includes the refuge on Upper Klamath Lake, just over the border in Oregon. The three are linked, perhaps fatefully, by a shared water supply, and they lie like small islands in a great sea of surrounding farmlands – land reclaimed by drainage and stream diversion from an original waterfowl paradise of marsh and open water. These farmlands around the refuges are now irrigated by water from Upper Klamath Lake. The irrigation waters, having been re-collected from the fields they have served, are pumped into Tule Lake and from there into Lower Klamath Lake. In the summer of 1960, biologists picked up hundreds of dead and dying birds at Tule Lake and Lower Klamath Lake. Most of them were fish-eating species – herons, pelicans, grebes, gulls. Upon analysis, they were found to contain insecticide residues identified as the chlorinated hydrocarbons toxaphene, DDD, and DDE. Fish from the lakes were also found to contain the insecticide residues; so were samples of plankton. It appears that pesticide residues are now building up in the waters of these refuges, being conveyed there by return irrigation flow from heavily sprayed agricultural lands. The refuges are critically important to the conservation of Western waterfowl. They lie in a strip of territory corresponding to the narrow neck of a funnel, in which all the migratory paths constituting what is known as the Pacific Flyway converge. During the fall migration, the three refuges receive many millions of ducks and geese, from nesting grounds that extend from the shores of the Bering Sea east to Hudson Bay – in fact, fully three-fourths of all the waterfowl that move south into or through the Pacific Coast states in autumn. During the summer, the refuges provide nesting areas for waterfowl, and especially for two endangered species, the redhead and the ruddy duck. If the lakes and pools of these refuges become seriously contaminated, the damage to the waterfowl populations of the Far West could be irreparable.

Water, of course, supports long chains of life – from the small-as-dust green cells of the drifting plant plankton, through the minute water fleas, to the fish that strain plankton from the water and are, in turn, eaten by other fish or by birds, mink, raccoons, and man himself, in an endless transfer of materials from life to life. We know that the minerals necessary for all these forms of life are extracted from the water and passed from link to link of the food chains. Can we suppose that poisons we introduce into water will not follow the same course? The answer is to be found in the recent history of Clear Lake, California. Clear Lake lies in mountainous country some ninety miles north of San Francisco and has long been popular with anglers. The name is plainly inappropriate; actually the lake is rather turbid, because its bottom, which is shallow, is covered with soft black ooze. Unfortunately for the fishermen and the resort dwellers on its shores, its waters have long provided an ideal habitat for a small gnat, *Chaoborus astictopus*. Although the gnat is closely related to mosquitoes, it is not a bloodsucker; indeed, it probably does not feed at all as an adult. However, the human beings who came to share its habitat found it annoying, because of its sheer numbers. Efforts were made to control it, but they were largely fruitless until, in the late nineteen-forties, the chlorinated-hydrocarbon insecticides offered a new weapon. The chemical chosen for a fresh attack was DDD, an insecticide that apparently offered fewer threats to fish life than DDT. The new control measures, undertaken in September of 1949, were carefully planned, and few people would have supposed that any harm could result. The lake was surveyed, its volume was determined, and the insecticide was applied in the concentration of one part to every seventy million parts of water. Control of the gnats was good at first, but by September of 1954 the treatment had to be repeated, and this time the chemical was added in the concentration of one part in fifty million parts of water. The destruction of the gnats was then thought to be virtually complete. The following winter months brought the first intimation that other life was affected; the western grebes on the lake began to die, and soon more than a hundred of them had been reported dead. At Clear Lake, the western grebe is a breeding bird and also a winter visitant, attracted by the abundant fish of the lake. It is a bird of spectacular appearance and beguiling habits, building floating nests in shallow lakes of the western United States and western Canada. It is sometimes called the 'swan grebe,' and with reason, for it glides with scarcely a ripple across the lake surface, its body riding low and its white neck and shining black head held high. The newly hatched chick is clothed in soft gray down; only a few hours after emerging from the shell it takes to the water, riding on the back of the father or mother, nestled under the parental wing coverts. Following a third assault on the ever-resilient gnat population, in September, 1957 – again in a concentration of one part of DDD to fifty million parts of water – more grebes died. Both then and in 1954, no evidence of infectious disease could be discovered on examination of the dead birds. But when someone thought of analyzing the fatty tissues of the grebes, they were found to be loaded with DDD in the extraordinary concentration of sixteen hundred parts per million. How could the chemical have built up to such prodigious levels? The grebes, of course, are fish eaters. When the fish of Clear Lake were also analyzed, the picture began to take form: the poison had been picked up by the smallest organisms, concentrated, and passed on to the larger ones, which concentrated it further. Plankton organisms were found to contain about five parts per million of the insecticide; plankton-eating fish had built up accumulations ranging from forty to three hundred parts per million; carnivorous species of fish had stored the most of all. One fish, a brown bullhead, had the astounding concentration of twenty-five hundred parts per million. It was a house-that-Jack-built sequence, in which the large carnivores had eaten the smaller carnivores, which had eaten the herbivores, which had eaten the plankton, which had absorbed the poison from the water.

Even more extraordinary discoveries were made later. No trace of DDD could be found in the water shortly after the last application of the chemical. But the poison had not really left the lake; it had merely gone into the fabric of the life that the lake supported. Twenty-three months after the chemical treatment had ceased, the plankton still contained as much as 5.3 parts of it per million. In that interval of nearly two years, successive crops of plankton had flowered and faded away, but the poison had somehow passed from generation to generation. And it lived on in the animal life of the lake as well. All fish, birds, and frogs examined a year after the chemical applications had ceased still contained DDD. The amount found in the flesh always exceeded by many times the original concentration in the water. Among these living carriers were fish that had hatched nine months after the last application of DDD. California gulls had built up concentrations of more than two thousand parts per million. The grebes still carried heavy residues, and meanwhile their nesting colonies had dwindled, from more than a thousand pairs before the first insecticide treatment to about thirty pairs in 1960. Even the thirty seem to have nested in vain, for no young grebes have been observed on the lake since the last DDD application. And what of the human being who has rigged his fishing tackle, caught a string of fish from the waters of Clear Lake, and taken them home to fry for supper? What could a heavy dose of DDD – and perhaps repeated heavy doses – do to him? The California State Department of Public Health professed to see no hazard, yet in 1959 it required that the use of DDD in the lake be stopped. In view of the evidence, the action seems a minimum safety measure.

The thin layer of soil that forms a patchy covering over the continents controls our own existence and that of every other animal of the land. Without soil, land plants as we know them could not grow, and without plants no animal could survive. Yet if our life depends on the soil, it is equally true that soil depends on life; its very origins and the maintenance of its true nature are intimately related to living plants and animals. For soil is in part a creation of life, born of a marvellous interaction of life and inert matter aeons ago. The parent materials were gathered together as volcanoes poured them out in fiery streams, as waters running over the bare rocks of the continents wore away even the hardest granite, and as the chisels of frost and ice split and shattered the rocks. Then living things began to work their creative magic, and little by little these inert materials became soil. Lichens, the rocks' first covering, aided the process of disintegration by means of acid secretions and made a lodging place for other life. Mosses took hold in these little pockets of simple soil – soil formed by crumbling bits of lichen, by the husks of minute insect life, by the debris of a fauna beginning its emergence from the sea. And not only did life help form the soil but living things now exist within it in incredible abundance and diversity; if this were not so, the soil would be a dead and sterile thing. The soil exists in a state of constant change, taking part in cycles that have no beginning and no end. New materials are constantly being contributed as rocks disintegrate, as organic matter decays, and as nitrogen and other gases are brought down in rain from the skies.

Simultaneously, materials are being taken away, harrowed temporarily for use by living creatures. Subtle and vastly important chemical changes are constantly in progress, converting elements derived from air and water into forms suitable for the support of plant life, and in all these changes living organisms are active agents.

There are few studies more fascinating, and at the same time more neglected, than the study of the teeming populations that exist in the dark realms of the soil. We know too little of the links that bind the soil organisms to each other, to their world, and to the world above. Perhaps the most essential organisms in the soil are the smallest – the invisible hosts of bacteria and of threadlike fungi. Statistics of their abundance take us at once into astronomical figures. A teaspoonful of topsoil may contain billions of bacteria. In spite of their minute size, the combined weight of bacteria in the top foot of a single acre of fertile soil, which itself weighs from ten to seventeen tons, may be as much as a thousand pounds. Ray fungi, growing in long filaments, are somewhat less numerous than the bacteria, but since they are larger, their total weight in a given amount of soil may be about the same. With small, green cells of algae, these make up the microscopic plant life of the soil. Bacteria, fungi, and algae are the principal agents of decay, reducing plant and animal residues to their component materials. The vast cyclic movements of chemical elements, such as carbon and nitrogen, through soil and air and living tissue could not proceed without these microplants. Without the nitrogen-fixing bacteria, for example, plants would starve for want of nitrogen, though they are surrounded by nitrogen-containing air. Other soil organisms form carbon dioxide, which on being dissolved in water becomes carbonic acid and aids in dissolving rock. Still other soil microbes perform the various oxidations and reductions by which minerals such as iron, manganese, and sulphur are transformed and made available to plants. Also present in prodigious numbers in the soil are microscopic mites and primitive, wingless insects called springtails. Small as they are, both play an important part in breaking down the residues of plants, and thus aid in the slow conversion of the litter of the forest floor to soil. The specialization of some of these minute creatures for their task is almost incredible. Several species of mites, for example, can begin life only within needles that have fallen from a spruce tree. Sheltered there, they digest out the inner tissues of the needle. By the time the mites have completed their development, only the outer layer of cells remains. The truly staggering task of dealing with the tremendous amount of plant material in the annual leaf fall belongs to some of the small insects of the soil and the forest floor. They macerate and digest the leaves, and help to mix the decomposed matter with the surface soil.

Besides all this horde of minute but ceaselessly toiling creatures, there are, of course, many larger forms, for soil life runs the gamut from bacteria to mammals. Some of these larger forms are permanent residents of the dark, subsurface layers; some hibernate or spend certain parts of their life cycles in underground chambers; some come and go freely between their burrows and the upper world. In general, the effect of all this habitation of the soil is to aerate it and to improve both its drainage and the penetration of water throughout the layers of plant growth. Of all the larger inhabitants of the soil, probably none is more important than the earth-worm. Just over three-quarters of a century ago, Charles Darwin published a book titled 'The Formation of Vegetable Mould Through the Action of Worms, with Observations on Their Habits.' In it he gave the world its first understanding of the fundamental role that earthworms play as geological agents for the transport of soil – a picture of surface rocks being gradually covered by fine soil brought up from below by the worms, which ingest earth in building burrows and as food and eject it near the surface in annual amounts running to many tons to the acre in the most favorable areas. At the same time, they draw quantities of organic matter contained in leaves and grass – as much as twenty pounds to the square yard in six months – down into the burrows, where they become part of the soil. Darwin's calculations showed that the toil of earthworms might produce a layer of soil from an inch to an inch and a half thick in a ten-year period. This is by no means all they do. Their burrows aerate the soil, keep it well drained, and aid the penetration of plant roots. And organic matter is broken down as it passes through their digestive tracts, so the soil is enriched by their excretory products.

What happens to the inhabitants of the soil when poisonous chemicals are carried down into their world, either introduced directly as soil 'sterilants' or sprayed on crops or borne by rain that has picked up a lethal contamination as it filtered through the leaf canopy of forest and orchard and cropland? Is it reasonable to suppose that a so-called broad-spectrum insecticide can kill the burrowing larval stages of a crop-destroying insect without also killing the insects whose function may be the essential one of breaking down organic matter? Or can we use a non-specific fungicide in orchards without also killing the fungi that inhabit the roots of many trees and aid the tree in extracting nutrients from the soil? The plain truth is that this critically important subject of the ecology of the soil has been largely neglected even by scientists and almost completely ignored by control men. The chemical control of insects seems to have proceeded on the assumption that the soil could and would sustain any amount of insult without striking back. From the few studies that have been made, a picture of the impact of pesticides on the soil is slowly emerging. The studies are not always in agreement, for soil types vary enormously and what causes damage in one may be innocuous in another. Light, sandy soils suffer far more heavily than humus types, for example, and combinations of chemicals often seem to do more harm than separate applications. Despite the varying results, enough solid evidence of harm is accumulating to cause apprehension on the part of the scientists concerned.

Under some conditions, the chemical conversions and transformations that lie at the very heart of the living world are affected. For example, the herbicide 2,4-D causes a temporary interruption of nitrification. Recent experiments in Florida showed that three chlorinated hydrocarbons – heptachlor, BHC (benzene hexachloride), and lindane, which is an isomer of BHC – reduced nitrification after only two weeks in the soil; BHC and DDT had significantly detrimental effects a year after treatment. In other experiments, it was found that BHC, lindane, aldrin, heptachlor, and DDD all prevented nitrogen-fixing bacteria from forming the necessary root nodules on leguminous plants, and also that a curious but beneficial relation between fungi and the roots of higher plants was seriously disrupted. Sometimes the problem is one of upsetting that delicate balance of populations by which nature accomplishes far-reaching aims. Explosive increases in certain kinds of soil organisms have occurred when other kinds have been reduced by insecticides, disturbing the relation of predator to prey. Such changes could easily alter the metabolic activity of the soil and affect its productivity. They could also mean that potentially harmful organisms, formerly held in check, might take on the status of pests.

One of the most important things to remember about insecticides in soil is their persistence. Aldrin has been recovered after four years, both as traces and, more abundantly, as converted to dieldrin. Ten years after the application of toxaphene to sandy soil, enough remains to kill termites. BHC persists a least eleven years, and heptachlor at least nine. Chlordane has been recovered after twelve years. Seemingly moderate applications of insecticides over a period of years may build up fantastic quantities in soil. The legend that 'a pound of DDT to the acre is harmless' means nothing if spraying is repeated. Potato soils have been found to contain up to fifteen pounds of DDT per acre, corn soils up to nineteen. A cranberry bog under study contained thirty-four and a half pounds to the acre. Soils from apple orchards seem to reach the peak of contamination, for the rate at which DDT accumulates here almost keeps pace with its rate of annual application. In a single season, if orchards are sprayed four or more times, DDT residues may amount to as much as fifty pounds to the acre. Arsenic provides a classic instance of the virtually permanent poisoning of the soil. Although since the mid-forties arsenic as a spray on growing tobacco has been largely replaced by the synthetic insecticides, the arsenic content of cigarettes made from American-grown tobacco increased more than three hundred per cent between the years 1932 and 1962. Dr. Henry S. Satterlee, an authority on arsenic toxicology, says that the soils of tobacco plantations are now thoroughly impregnated with arsenic residues in the form of a heavy and relatively insoluble poison, arsenate of lead. This will continue to release arsenic in soluble form.

As Dr. Satterlee puts it, the soil of a large proportion of the land planted with tobacco has been
subjected to 'cumulative and well-nigh permanent poisoning.' Tobacco grown in the eastern
Mediterranean countries, where arsenical insecticides are not used, has shown no such increase
in arsenic content.

The question arises to what extent insecticides
are absorbed into plant tissues from contaminated soils. Much depends on the type of soil,
the crop, and the nature and the concentration
of the insecticide. Soils high in organic matter
release smaller quantities of poisons than others
do. Carrots absorb more insecticide than any
other crop studied; if the insecticide used happens to be lindane, carrots actually accumulate
higher concentrations than are present in the soil.
In the future, it may become necessary to analyze
soils for insecticides before planting certain food
crops. Otherwise, unsprayed crops may take up
enough insecticide from the soil to render them
unfit for market. This very sort of contamination
has already created endless problems for at least
one leading manufacturer of baby foods, who has
been unwilling to buy any fruits or vegetables

that have been exposed to insecticides. The chemical that caused him the most trouble was BHC, which is taken up by the roots and tubers of plants, and which advertises its presence by a musty taste and odor. Sweet potatoes grown in California fields where BHC had been used two years earlier contained residues, and the firm had to reject them. Another year, in which the firm had contracted for its total requirements of sweet potatoes with growers in South Carolina, so large a proportion of the acreage was found to be contaminated that the company was forced to buy in the open market, at a considerable financial loss. The manufacturer's most stubborn problem has been with peanuts. In the Southern states, peanuts are usually grown in rotation with cotton, on which BHC is extensively used, and the peanuts pick up considerable amounts of the insecticide. Actually, only a trace is enough to give them the telltale musty odor and taste. The chemical penetrates the nuts and cannot be removed.

Sometimes the menace is to the crop itself – a menace as long-lasting as the insecticide contamination of the soil. Some insecticides affect sensitive plants such as beans, wheat, barley, and rye, retarding root development or inhibiting the growth of seedlings. The experience of the hop growers of Washington and Idaho is an example. During the spring of 1955, many of these growers undertook a large-scale program to control the strawberry-root weevil, whose larvae had become abundant on the roots of the hops. On the advice of agricultural experts and insecticide manufacturers, they chose heptachlor to do the job. Within a year after the heptachlor was applied, in both dust and spray forms, the vines in the treated yards were wilting and dying. In the untreated fields there was no trouble; in fact, the damage stopped at the border between treated and untreated fields. The fields were replanted, at great expense, but the next year the new roots, too, were found to be dead. Four years later, the soil still contained heptachlor, and scientists were unable to predict how long it would remain poisonous, or to recommend any procedure for correcting the condition. The United States Department of Agriculture, which as late as March, 1959, had declared heptachlor to be acceptable for use on hops in the form of a soil treatment, thereafter belatedly withdrew its registration for such use. Meanwhile, the hop growers sought what redress they could in the courts.

In continuing to contaminate the soil, we are almost certainly headed for trouble. This was the consensus of a groups of specialists who met in 1960 at the College of Forestry of the State University of New York, in Syracuse, to discuss the ecology of the soil. These men summed up the hazards of using 'such potent and little understood tools' as chemicals and radioactive substances: 'A few false moves on the part of man may result in destruction of soil productivity and the arthropods may well take over.'

Water, soil, and the earth's green mantle of plants make up the world that supports the animal life of the earth. Although modern man seldom remembers the fact, he could not exist without the plants that harness the sun's energy and manufacture the basic foodstuffs he depends upon for life. Our attitude toward plants is a singularly narrow one. If we see any immediate utility in a plant, we foster it. If, for any reason, we find its presence undesirable, or even simply a matter of indifference, we may condemn it to destruction forthwith. Besides the various plants that are poisonous to man or his livestock, or crowd out food plants, many are marked for destruction merely because they happen to be in the wrong place at the wrong time, and many others are destroyed merely because they happen to be associates of the unwanted plants. Sometimes we have no choice but to disturb the relationships between plants and the earth, between plants and other plants, and between plants and animals, yet we should do so thoughtfully, with full awareness that what we do may have consequences remote in time and place.

One example of our unthinking bludgeoning of the landscape is to be seen in the sagebrush lands of the West, where a vast campaign has been launched to destroy the sage and substitute grass. If ever an enterprise needed to be illuminated with a sense of the history and meaning of the landscape, it is this one. For here the natural landscape is eloquent of the interplay of forces that have created it. It is spread before us like the pages of an open book, telling why the land is what it is, and why we should preserve its integrity. But the pages lie unread. The land of the sage is the land of the high Western plains and the lower slopes of the mountains that rise above them – a land born of the uplift of the Rocky Mountain system many millions of years ago. It is a place of harsh extremes of climate: of long winters when blizzards drive down from the mountains and snow lies thick on the plains, of summers whose heat is relieved only by scanty rains, with drought biting deep into the soil, and dry winds stealing moisture from leaf and stem. In the evolution of this landscape, there must have been a long period of trial and error as plants attempted the colonization of the high and wind-swept land. One after another must have failed. At last, a group of plants took root that combined all the qualities needed for survival. The sage – low-growing and shrubby – could maintain its hold on the mountain slopes and on the plains, and within its small gray leaves it could store moisture enough to defy the thieving winds. It was no accident but, rather, the result of long ages of experimentation by nature that the great plains of the West became the land of the sage.

Along with the plants, animal life was evolving in harmony with the searching requirements of the land. In time there were two animals as well adjusted to their habitat as the sage. One was a mammal, the fleet and graceful pronghorn antelope. The other was a bird, the sage grouse – the 'cock of the plains' of Lewis and Clark. The sage and the grouse seem made for each other. The range of the bird coincides with the range of the sage, and the sage is all things to these birds of the plains. The low sage of the foothill ranges shelters their nests and their young; the denser growths are loafing and roosting areas; at all times the sage provides the staple food of the grouse. Yet it is a two-way relationship. The spectacular courtship displays of the cocks help loosen the soil beneath and around the sage, aiding invasion by grasses that can grow in the shelter of the sagebrush. The antelope, too, have adjusted their lives to the sage. Though some of them summer in the mountains, they are primarily animals of the plains, and in winter, when the first snows come, they all seek the lower elevations. There the sage provides the food that tides them over the winter. Where all other plants have shed their leaves, the gray-green leaves of the sage – bitter, aromatic, rich in proteins, fats, and needed minerals – cling to the stems of the densely growing plants. Though the snows pile up, the tops of the sage remain exposed, or can be reached by the sharp, pawing hoofs of the antelope. Then grouse feed on them, too, finding them on bare and windswept ledges or following the antelope to spots where they have scratched away the snow. Other life also looks to the sage. Mule deer often feed on it. Sage may mean survival to winter-grazing livestock. Sheep graze many winter ranges where the big sage brush forms almost pure stands. For half the year, it is their principal forage, and it is a plant of higher energy value than even alfalfa hay.

The upland plains, the purple wastes of sage, the wild, swift antelope, and the grouse are then a natural system in perfect balance. Or, rather, in many places, there was such a balance. In recent years, the land-management agencies have set about satisfying the insatiable demands of the cattlemen for more grazing land. By this they mean grassland – grass without sage. Few seem to have asked whether grassland is a stable and desirable goal in the region. Certainly nature's own answer was no. The annual precipitation in this land is not enough to support good sod-forming grass; rather, it favors the bunch grass that grows in the shelter of the sage. Yet millions of acres of sage-brush lands are sprayed each year. What are the results? The long-term effects of eliminating sage and seeding with grass are largely conjectural. Men of long experience in the ways of the land say that in this country there is better growth of grass between and under the moisture-holding sage than can possibly be had in pure stands. But even if the program succeeds in its immediate objective, it is clear that the whole closely knit fabric of life is being ripped apart. The antelope and the grouse will disappear, along with the sage. Even the live-stock, which are the intended beneficiaries, will suffer; no amount of lush green grass in summer can help the sheep starving in the winter storms for lack of the sage and bitter brush and other wild vegetation of the plains. These are the first and obvious effects. Others are of the kind that is always associated with the shotgun approach to nature: the spraying also eliminates a great many plants that were not its intended target. Justice William O. Douglas, in his recent book 'My Wilderness: East to Katahdin,' has told of an example of ecological destruction wrought by the Forest Service in the Bridger National Forest, in

Wyoming. Yielding to the pressure of cattlemen for more grassland, the Service sprayed some ten thousand acres of sage lands. The sage was killed, as was intended. But so was a green, life-giving ribbon of willows that traced its way across these plains, following the meandering streams. Moose had lived in these willow thickets, for willow is to the moose what sage is to the antelope. Beavers had lived there, too, feeding on the willows, felling them, and making strong dams across the tiny streams. Through the labor of the beavers, a lake backed up. Trout in the mountain streams were seldom more than six inches long; in the lake they thrived so prodigiously that many grew to five pounds. Waterfowl were attracted to the lake. But with the 'improvement' instituted by the Forest Service, the willows went the way of the sagebrush, killed by the same, impartial spray. When Justice Douglas visited the area in 1959, the year of the spraying, he was shocked to see the shrivelled and dying willows – the 'vast, incredible damage.' What would become of the moose? Of the beavers and the little world they had constructed? A year later, he returned to read the answers in the devastated landscape. The moose were gone, and so were the beavers. The principal beaver dam had gone out for want of attention by its skilled architects, and the lake had drained away. None of the large trout were left, for none could live in the tiny creek that remained, threading its way through a bare, hot land.

Besides the more than four million acres of range lands sprayed each year, large areas of other types of land are potential or actual recipients of chemical treatments for weed control. For example, in the United States an area larger than all of New England – some fifty million acres – is under the management of utility corporations, and much of it is routinely treated for 'brush control.' In the Southwest, an estimated seventy-five million acres of mesquite lands require management by some means, and chemical spraying is the method most actively pushed. An unknown but very large acreage of timber-producing lands is now aerially sprayed for the purpose of 'weeding out' the hardwoods from the more spray-resistant conifers. Added to these are an estimated fifty-three million acres of agricultural lands, perhaps two million acres of non-crop lands, and countless private lawns, parks, and golf courses, the combined acreage of which must reach an extremely large figure. And besides all this, there are our roadsides.

Roadside brush control is practiced in all parts of the country, with the object of eliminating plants that ultimately grow tall enough to obstruct drivers' vision or to interfere with wires on rights of way. This is a legitimate object, but as roadside spraying is commonly carried out, it has many undesirable side effects. One of them is economic. The town fathers of a thousand communities lend willing ears to the chemical salesmen and the eager contractors who will rid their roadsides of 'brush.' Spraying, they are told, is cheaper than mowing. So, perhaps, it appears in the neat rows of figures in the official books, but were the true cost entered, the wholesale broadcasting of chemicals would be seen to be far more expensive, both in dollars and in the infinite damage it does. Take, for example, a commodity that is prized by every chamber of commerce throughout the land – the good will of vacationing tourists. There is a steadily growing chorus of outraged protest at the disfigurement of once beautiful roadsides by chemical sprays. 'We are making a dirty, brown,

dying-looking mess along the sides of our roads,'
a New England woman wrote angrily to her local
newspaper last fall. 'This is not what the tourists expect, with all the money we are spending
advertising the beautiful scenery.' In the summer
of 1960, conservationists from many states con-
verged on a beautiful Maine island to witness its
presentation to the National Audubon Society by
its owner, Millicent Todd Bingham. The focus
that day was on the preservation of the natural
landscape, with its intricate web of life whose
interwoven strands lead from microbe to man.
But in the background of all the conversations
among the visitors to the island was indignation
at the despoiling of the roads they had travelled
to reach it. Once, it had been a joy to follow those
roads through the evergreen forests – roads lined
with bayberry and sweet fern, alder and huckleberry. Now all was brown desolation. One of the
conservationists wrote of that summer pilgrim-
age, 'I returned . . . angry at the desecration of
the Maine roadsides. Where, in previous years,
the highways were bordered with wild flowers
and attractive shrubs, there were only the scars
of dead vegetation for mile after mile. . . . As an

economic proposition, can Maine afford the loss of tourist good will that such sights induce?'

Botanists at the Connecticut Arboretum, in New London, declare that the elimination of beautiful native shrubs and wild flowers has reached the proportions of a 'roadside crisis.' Azaleas, mountain laurel, blueberry, huckleberry, viburnum, dogwood, hayberry, sweet fern, low shadbush, winterberry, chokecherry, and wild plum are dying under the chemical barrage. So are the daisies, the black-eyed Susans, the Queen Anne's lace, the goldenrod, and the fall asters. In the spring of 1957, trees within the Connecticut Arboretum Natural Area were seriously injured when the town of Waterford sprayed the road-sides with chemical weed killers. Even large trees not directly sprayed were affected. The leaves of the oaks began to curl and turn brown, although it was the season for spring growth. Then new shoots appeared, and these grew with abnormal rapidity, giving a 'weeping' appearance to the trees. Two seasons later, large branches on some of these trees had died, other branches were with-out leaves, and the deformed, weeping effect of whole trees persisted.

I know well a stretch of road where nature's own landscaping once provided a border of alder, viburnum, sweet fern, and juniper, with seasonally changing accents of bright flowers, and of fruits hanging in jewelled clusters in the fall. The road had no heavy load of traffic to support, and there were few sharp curves or intersections where brush could obstruct the driver's vision. Nevertheless, the sprayers took over, and the miles along that road became something to be traversed quickly, a sight to be endured with one's mind closed to thoughts of the sterile and hideous world we are letting our technicians make. Here and there, though, authority had faltered, and by an unaccountable oversight there were oases of beauty – oases that made the desecration of the greater part of the road the more unbearable. In such places, my spirit lifted to the sight of the drifts of white clover or the clouds of purple vetch, with here and there the flaming cup of a wood lily. Such plants are 'weeds' only to those who make a business of selling and applying weed killers.

There is, of course, more to the wish to preserve our roadside vegetation than aesthetic considerations. In the economy of nature, the natural vegetation has its essential place. Hedge-rows along country roads and the edges of fields provide food, cover, and nesting areas for birds and homes for many small animals; indeed, of some seventy species of shrubs and vines that are typical roadside species, about sixty-five are important to wildlife as food. Such vegetation is also the habitat of wild bees and other polli-nating insects. Man is more dependent on these wild pollinators than he usually realizes. Even the farmer seldom understands the value of wild bees, and often participates in measures that rob him of their services. Not only many wild plants but some agricultural crops are partly or wholly dependent on the services of the native pollinat-ing insects; several hundred species of wild bees take part in the pollination of cultivated crops – a hundred species visiting the flowers of alfalfa alone. Moreover, in the absence of insect pollina-tion, most of the soil-holding and soil-enriching plants of uncultivated areas would die out, with far-reaching consequences for the ecology of the whole region. A great variety of herbs, shrubs, and trees of our forests and ranges depend on native insects for their reproduction, and without these plants many wild animals and much range stock would find little food. Now 'clean' cultivation and the chemical spraying of hedgerows and weeds, including some of those that bees depend upon heavily for food, are eliminating the last sanctuaries of these pollinating insects and thereby breaking the threads that bind life to life. The bees, so essential to our agriculture and indeed to our landscape as we know it, deserve something better from us than the senseless destruction of their habitat.

Ironically, the all-out chemical assault perpetuates the problems it seeks to correct. Ragweed, the bane of hayfever sufferers, offers an interesting example of the way efforts to control nature sometimes boomerang. Many thousands of gallons of chemicals have been discharged along roadsides in the name of ragweed control, but the unfortunate truth is that blanket spraying is resulting in more ragweed, not less. Ragweed is an annual; each year its seedlings require open soil in order to become established. Our best protection against this plant is therefore the maintenance of dense shrubs and ferns and other perennial vegetation. Spraying destroys this protective vegetation and creates open, barren areas, which the ragweed hastens to fill.

Just as ironically, some spraying actually creates new problems. The chemical 2,4-D, by killing out the broad-leaved plants, allows the grasses to thrive, and now some of the grasses themselves have become 'weeds,' presenting a new problem of control and giving the cycle another turn. This situation is acknowledged in a recent issue of a technical journal devoted to crop problems, which notes that 'with the widespread use of 2,4-D to control broad-leaved weeds, grass weeds in particular have increasingly become a threat to corn and soybean yields.'

We persist in this inefficient approach despite the fact that a perfectly sound method of selective spraying is known, which can achieve long-term vegetational control and eliminate repeated spraying of most types of vegetation. Selective spraying was developed by Dr. Frank Egler, a plant ecologist who was for some years associated with the American Museum of Natural History and who is the chairman of a Committee for Brush Control Recommendations for Rights of Way. The method he devised takes advantage of the fact that the best and cheapest controls for vegetation are not chemicals but other plants. Trees find it difficult to gain a foothold in a community of shrubs, and on roadsides most shrubs, and all ferns and wild flowers, are low enough to present no hazard to drivers and no obstruction to wires. Selective spraying, in contrast to blanket spraying, is directed only at trees and exceptionally tall shrubs, the poison being applied at the base. (Cutting down a tree is seldom a permanent solution, because many trees will grow again.) One spraying may be sufficient to eliminate such trees and shrubs, with a possible followup for extremely resistant species; thereafter the shrubs assert control and the trees do not return. Dr. Egler has under observation shrub communities that have remained stable, without return of trees, for a quarter of a century after selective spraying. The spraying can often be done by men on foot, with knapsack sprayers, which give them complete control over their material. Sometimes tanks and compressor pumps can be mounted on truck chassis, but there is still no blanket spraying. The integrity of the environment is thereby preserved, the enormous value of the wildlife habitat remains intact, and the beauty of shrub and fern and the rest of the roadside growth has not been sacrificed. The method of vegetation management by selective spraying has been adopted by the authorities in some areas. All other considerations aside, when more taxpayers understand that the bill for spraying the town roads should come due only once a generation instead of once a year, they will surely rise up and demand a change of method.

The chemical pesticides are a bright new toy. They sometimes work in a spectacular way, giving those who wield them a giddy sense of power over nature, and as for the failures and the long-range undesirable effects, these are dismissed as the baseless imaginings of pessimists. Disregarding the whole record of contamination and death, we continue to spray, and to spray indiscriminately. We proceed as if there were no alternative, even though there are alternatives, such as biological controls and selective spraying, which have been effective in many places. As Dr. C. J. Brièjer, a Dutch scientist of rare understanding, has put it, 'We are walking in nature like an elephant in the china cabinet.'